KICK-START YOUR SALON INTO PROFIT

Take Control & Turn Your Business Around In 10 Steps!

EGO IWEGBU-DALEY

Thank you...
Colin, Rachel, Margaret, Boris, Mum and Dad

Published by Agushka Publishing, London

Agushka Publishing

+44 (0) 845 643 1619

First Edition 2009

ISBN
978-0-9560351-3-4
Kick-Start Your Salon Into Profit (Paperback)

HELLO

Here's a fact... many large organisations owe their continued top performance to assistance from external consultants and experts; so with that in mind don't feel embarrassed about seeking help for your salon. So many salon owners and managers feel under pressure to have all the answers and be in charge all the time. It's easy to forget that just like your team, you too need encouragement and direction from time-to-time. Whilst you clearly had to have been a self-starter to be where you are today sometimes just being able to talk to someone who understands your business can be such a relief!

If you have found yourself in a viscous circle of constantly making marginal returns, just enough to meet payroll and rent, then by now you might be tired, disheartened, or even bored of the daily grind of running your salon business. You may even have started entertaining thoughts of selling the business, or worse just 'shutting-up shop' and walking away! "This isn't what you imagined it would be!" When you first started you thought you would open this fabulous salon, customers would come flocking in, your professional team of staff would happily show up, smiling everyday to work and your till would be ringing with the sound of profit, profit and more profit! Instead you're finding yourself working day and night either on the shop floor or in the office, many of your team have disappointed you in the past, clients come and go and the takings are less than expected. You're thinking, "I work so hard; this is just not fair! Did I bite off more than I can chew?"

Well, you've just learnt the hard way that the salon business is actually quite complex and is not just a straightforward 'buy and sell' type of business. There are so many important aspects that need to be right to be truly successful – staffing, retailing, merchandising, marketing, training, customer service, hygiene, treatment methods, stock selection and management, financial management, client and business record management, health & safety and the general management of the daily operations. A long list, but funnily, as complex as this business is and how diverse the set of skills required to do a good job, most people start salons on their own! Meaning, you, alone are in charge of the whole show! Phew! No wonder it has been tough!

So, I say, give yourself a pat on the back for making it this far and an even bigger pat for seeking help! You've done so much to get to this point and this ***Kick-Start Your Salon Into Profit Booklet*** will give you a new way of seeing your salon, providing the kind of clarity that may have been lost (or never had) over time. Follow this guide and get your salon making money while you have more freedom!

PS - Gentlemen readers - Please excuse the fact that I mostly use female terms in this booklet; I still mean to address men as well!

MORE HELP!

Miss Salon™ - The Salon Business Consultants aim to provide the kind of help that empowers salon owners and managers to take control of their business. Our services include step-by-step DIY guides to power workshops, from interim management to just providing a sounding board for your thoughts and ideas. We have worked with many big brands, launching salons, staffing, training, planning beauty events and providing unique marketing solutions. **Our clients include Superdrug, Revlon, Bourjois, Crabtree&Evelyn, Clothes Show Live, London Fashion Week-End, Topshop, Selfridges&Co and more.** We are proud to say that our business has grown through word-of-mouth, so visit our site to read what they say about us - www.misssalon.com.

EGO IWEGBU-DALEY

I have been in the industry for 10 years; I have experienced super highs and super lows. I've owned 6 salons, some hugely successful and some not, and learnt all my lessons the hard way. I was so busy all day every day that I never had time to stop and plan, analyze and strategize. I wished I had a mentor and a guide.

I came away from my salon days with a huge amount of experience and knowledge; I know what I did that got one salon generating £330k and another (same size) making only £78k!

My personal business experiences and those of my clients have lead me to understand that the best approach to achieving long-term success is a strategic one; a methodical plan which ***looks-at and keeps-in-check all elements of your business***. I developed this 10-Step Action Plan to increasing profitability having successfully helped others with their business ventures. It will take you through a diagnostic approach, looking at key elements of your business, finally uncovering important opportunities for improvement.

1-DAY POWER WORKSHOP

To accompany this guide I have also created an inspirational, informative and interactive power workshop. You will be able to network with other salon owners whilst following a structured 1-day programme of tutorials, discussions, examples and more - all designed to empower you to drive your salon business forward. Book your place today! Call Miss Salon™ on 0845 643 1619.

CONTENT

WHY DO SO MANY SMALL BUSINESSES FAIL?

In general this boils down to the following 4 reasons:-

1. The owner of the business (salon) is one of its best or main operators - meaning you are always on the shop floor and have a long list of clients that will not go to anyone else.

2. The business was started with not enough money – you started your salon with just enough money to open its doors; no backup funds for cash flow lows or budgets for marketing, pr, training, business coaching, unexpected costs, etc.

3. The business owner is inexperienced and has no experienced support through business mentors and coaches or through an experienced board of directors – you may have thought that there's not much to running your own shop, after-all, it's not rocket science… anyone can do it! Or maybe you thought, I love doing hair, nails or facials and I'm really good at it, so I'll just open my own shop – I already know the business!

"Be more strategic and methodical in the way you operate"

4. Lack of proper planning – no business plan, no marketing plan, no pr plan, no operations manual, no training manual, no staff handbook, no company policy, no customer service policy… basically no strategy and no clear plan for success!

Let's face it, most small business owners are notorious for not preparing proper plans. Writing business plans, marketing plans, creating operations manuals and so on all seem over-the-top and not like real business; just a load of paperwork and theory. Whilst I agree that one of the greatest skills a business owner has is the ability to 'get-on' and make things happen in the 'real world', it must be said that taking some time out to thoroughly work through a strategy and write down some plans can save a lot of 'headless chicken' actions! The salon business is a service business that must factor in the products and equipment used and the time taken to perform the treatments. It requires experienced and qualified staff and relies on continuous and consistent customer satisfaction. Not having a mapped-out strategy for success means it is open to all sorts of potentially 'door-shutting' mistakes at worst or just on-going mediocre sales at best! Never maximising on strengths and minimising weaknesses; never making informed decisions about what opportunities to grab and which ones to let go.

So in order for you to turn your business around now and make the most of it you are going to have to start being much more strategic and methodical in the way you operate.

PART OF BEING MORE STRATEGIC...

So in order to keep everyone in your business thinking more strategically you will need to create a ***Strategy Statement***...

"*What?*" I hear you say. "Sounds like blah blah to me! I thought this book was about action... Not a load of old rhetoric!"

Well don't underestimate the power of rhetoric; well chosen, directional words can lead to action!

All you need is a simple statement that clearly defines what your business is ultimately trying to achieve and how it will go about doing this.

The strategy statement template

XY Salon aims to... [what] by offering... [what] to... [who] through... [how].

XY Salon aims to "turnover £250k in 2009 *by offering* affordable, fuss-free and convenient quick-fix beauty treatments and products *to* image-conscious, price-sensitive and time-poor passers-by, *through* a highly skilled team and a well maintained and merchandised salon and shop."

This 35-word statement has described many things about the business. The business has a tangible aim, has defined its product range (affordable, fuss-free, convenient); has defined its target market (image-conscious, price-sensitive, time-poor); has defined its booking policy (passers-by, therefore always ready for walk-ins); has defined its hiring and training policy (highly skilled team); and has defined its salon look.

If all of the important factors are properly considered when creating your strategy statement then you and your team can rely on it to keep your decisions and actions in-line with the businesses goal.

But before writing your strategy statement, read Steps 1 to 10...

STEP 1
WHAT DO YOUR CUSTOMERS WANT & NEED?

HAVE YOU DEFINED YOUR MARKET?

A market is the set of all actual and potential buyers of a product or service. You may have been in business for many years or just started your salon a few months ago, either way clearly defining who your service is for will help you reach that person much more easily, with targeted communications, treatments and products. With the seemingly growing number of salons on every high street, it is vital that you home-in on a set group and create a treatment and product list that is suited to their needs. Some of you may have had other salons open right next door or nearby and you no longer stand out as the only place to get a tan, manicure, etc It is at this point; with a clear target market, that you would do all you can to make yourself even more attractive to your specific audience! But how will you do this properly, without wasting time and money if you don't know who they are? Thinking about customer needs first – and then identifying the products that meet those needs – is the best way to define a market.

"Thinking about customer needs first – and then identifying the products that meet those needs – is the best way to define a market. "

So start by creating a list that describes the type of people that visits your salon or that you want to attract to your salon.

If you haven't quite chosen a typical customer or maybe you were one of those unfortunate salon owners who started your business thinking *everyone* would come to your shop (me included), then I would start by choosing the largest market in your area to target. Would the largest market be predominately tourists, busy shoppers, stay-at-home mums, high-income employed/self-employed, low-income employed/self-employed, unemployed and so on? The location of your premises will definitely help you get a better understanding of who are/will be the most likely users of your salon.

If you are still unsure of who the largest market in your area is then you will need to do some market research; this could include creating a focused questionnaire for your current clients or passers-by to complete. I know you're thinking, no one likes to fill out questionnaires... well I didn't say it was going to be easy! For your clients - tell them that you are planning on improving the salon and you would really appreciate if they could just tick the box that is most relevant to them; questionnaires are anonymous, will take just two minutes to complete and they'll receive 5% off their next visit. For passers-by, offer them chocolate for 2 minutes of their time, no strings! If you can get 100 women to answer 20 well thought-out questions you will start to get a really good picture of what they do, need and want from you! Try it today!!

HERE IS AN EXAMPLE OF A LIST DESCRIBING A PARTICULAR GROUP/PERSON:-

- Female
- Age 18-35
- Low-income part-time employed (supermarket cashier, cleaner, nursery worker)
- Unemployed (stay-home mums, housewives, on benefits/welfare)
- Enjoy popular celebrity culture (especially like people they can relate to like Coleen Rooney, Cheryl Cole, Katie Price)
- Enjoy popular reality TV shows
- Drink alcohol and enjoy regular nights out with friends
- Have dreams of wealth (play the lottery, bingo)
- Want to look as good as possible
- Can't afford, don't have time or don't really value treatments designed for well-being, detoxification and relaxation
- Prefer to go for treatments that show immediate results
- The salon is seen as a facilitator of a look rather than a place to unwind

(If you needed to do some market research to identify your customer - what questions would you need to ask in a simple questionnaire to gain this type of insight?)

So what is her need?

Popular, instant beauty-enhancing, affordable treatments - *her need is to look good fast - immediate results in quick time.* She will do as much as she can herself at home but she will find a salon to do the rest. Therefore her ideal salon would offer the following:-

Treatments
Nail enhancements
Manicure/Pedicure
Nail art
Tanning (spray and/or sun beds)
Hair highlights, extensions, straightening, blow-dry
Lash extensions/tint/perm
Waxing

Threading
Makeup
Skin aesthetics - Botox®, Fillers
Fat and water retention reduction
Teeth whitening

Extras
Massage
Facials

Environment
TV
Wine and fizzy drinks
Latest gossip magazines
Same age range staff

Sells
Earrings, party rings
Tanning creams
GHD Straighteners
Hair extension clips and other hair DIY kits
Hair accessories
Sunglasses
Magazine subscriptions
Makeup, especially lipgloss, glitter sprays, glitter liners
Quick dry topcoats, glitter topcoats, nail files
Fragrance, body sprays
Treatment aftercare products

(After doing this exercise, I would create a quick customer preference questionnaire, just to confirm that I have got her needs right. Example questions - Do you prefer to Walk-in or Make Appointment? What treatments interest you; please tick boxes (list treatments)? What's you preferred salon environment; TV, Peace & Quite, Pop Music, Radio, Soft Music? Are you interested in any of the following items (list types of retail items)? What magazines do you read? And so on...)

Provide your clients with what they want...

HERE ARE 3 MAIN NEEDS THAT SALONS AND SPAS FULFIL

Beauty Enhancing and Grooming
Instant (hair extensions, pedicure, hair removal, skin polish, hair-do, etc)
Requiring a series of treatments (cellulite reduction, acne treatment facials, etc)

Detoxification
Internal treatments (colonics, fasting, etc)
External treatments (sauna, salt scrubs, massage, etc)
Organic, holistic, homeopathic

Relaxation
Massages, reflexology
Frequent (day spas, health clubs)
Occasional (retreats, holidays)

ARE YOU FULFILLING YOUR CUSTOMERS NEEDS?

After you have thoroughly described your largest immediate market, take a look at your treatment menu and product list. Are you providing what they want? Are you offering too much - spending money where it's not really needed? Are you offering enough - maybe losing business because you don't provide a crucial treatment? Do this exercise and if there are changes to be made write your ideal treatment menu as if you were starting all over again. Put this down for now ... we will use this information in Step 7.

"High performing organisations are companies that create unique selling points, processes, prices, teams and offers that are focused on a customers need."

"As such, their acquisition and retention rates are high."

STEP 1
STOP | START | CONTINUE

STOP

- Adding treatments to your menu without proper thought and analysis - does your market actually want this treatment?
- Spending money on equipment and training for treatments that are irrelevant to your market.

START

- Perfecting and marketing the treatments that are interesting to your audience.
- Retailing items that complement your menu and are interesting and attractive to your audience.

CONTINUE

- To keep up-to-date with all the latest fashion, beauty and well-being trends.
- To speak to your customers, asking them what they are up to, how they feel about your services and whether they want to see any other treatments added to the list.

STEP 2
FIND THE GOOD THE BAD & THE UGLY!

THE SWOT ANALYSIS

Assess where you are and how strong your position is in the market by doing a SWOT analysis. This is a meticulous look at the **Strengths, Weaknesses, Opportunities and Threats** associated with your business. The Strengths and Weaknesses will be things that come from within your business and the Opportunities and Threats will be external factors that affect or may affect your business.

Here are some **EXAMPLES** of Strengths, Weaknesses, Opportunities and Threat:-

Strengths – What is really good about your salon business (internal)?

- High customer loyalty. Regular customers enjoy the benefits of the loyalty-points scheme offered by the salon with 70% uptake. (This is a strong indication of a relevant, well planned and executed marketing activity)

- High staff loyalty. Staff turnover is minimal at 70%; 4 out of 6 members are the same since the salon opened. (This is a strong indication of good management and an effective recruitment process)

- Excellent customer service. Having recently performed a customer survey, the business received top marks for customer service, hygiene and treatments. (This is a strong indication of good management)

- Shop located on a busy high street. The salon gets a lot of passing traffic and is visited on average by 3 new customers a day. (This is not really an internal attribute, however it shows good management decision in securing an ideal location for the business)

- Continued growth in spite of the competition. Even with two other salons within 5 minutes walking distance from the salon, business has shown steady year on year growth. (This is a strong indication of good management, customer service and marketing)

Other example strengths in brief...

- Salon owner/manager knows when to seek assistance or professional help.
- Salon has a great atmosphere; clients always seem to enjoy their visits.
- Management have clear policies in place.
- Staff and management have regular meetings; issues are aired and resolved quickly in an open and honest manner.
- Salon has a 'shopping area' for clients to browse.
- Salon has excellent technicians/operators.
- Only salon for 10 miles that offers spray tans (for example).

What are you doing daily to boost these strengths?

Weaknesses – What are its limitations? Where could it grow or do better (internal)?

- The business owner is the salons best and most popular therapist. This means they spend most of their time on the shop floor with clients and not enough time managing and marketing the business. This is being addressed by slowly moving her clients over to other excellent staff and not taking on any new clients.

- No parking; this is frustrating for some of the clients and may be preventing new customers in cars from popping in. Owner is currently in talks with a nearby office building and a local supermarket trying to negotiate some parking from them in exchange for staff (or even customer) discounts.

- Some staff members are more versatile than others; this means that certain treatments can only be performed by one staff member. This is being addressed through the Knowledge Sharing Hour Programme held in the salon every Wednesday afternoon; individual staff members do practical demonstrations of their skills while others watch, follow and practice.

- Underutilized first floor; the salon is on the ground floor but the building is on 2 floors. The first floor at the moment is used for storage but there is enough space to add another tanning booth and beauty room.

Other example weaknesses in brief...

- A weak approach to marketing and pr; hence very few new clients.
- Always experience poor/average product sales.
- Low cash reserves; business breaks even but has no budget for much else.
- Salon interior is out of date.
- Customers have difficulty finding the salon; salon isn't ideally located.
- Limited floor space; always a struggle to add new treatments.

What are you doing to solve these weaknesses?

Opportunities – What opportunities has your business been or could be presented with (external)?

- The first floor of the salon can be transformed into a tanning booth and treatment room. This will increase sales and reduce the number of clients that are turned away due to lack of space.

- The salon has been approached by a local business to provide their staff with a "beauty half hour" package on a weekly basis. This will increase sales and the customer base.

- Salon has a back garden; plan to host beauty garden parties in the summer.

- There is an opportunity to participate in a number of local mother and baby fairs; offering quick and easy treatments as part of an advertising campaign.

Other opportunities in brief...

- Salon has enough space to add a 'shopping area'.
- Could retail products online.
- Could create exclusivity by introducing an 'own-brand' range of products.
- Should introduce a wider variety of products to sell.
- Could rent out top floor.
- Could merchandise products more effectively.

What are you doing to capitalise on these opportunities?

Threats – What are the worst case scenarios for your business and how will you address them (external)?

- The 10 year lease expires in 2 years and the landlord may not renew it. The salon may have to relocate. However, commercial estate agents have been contacted to start the search for similar and even better premises.

- The country is in a recession; people are beginning to tighten their budgets. This is an opportunity to increase our market share by communicating to our market that their buck is better spent here; either because they get more for their money or that their intangible needs will be better met. Intangible needs such as comfort, brand association, convenience, etc. (We will talk more about marketing communications in Step 7)

- Salon will soon be in a congestion charge zone - drivers will be charged for entering the zone. This may not be that big a deal to your clients, but just incase you should investigate other methods of travel to your salon and maybe produce a friendly card that shows you care and empathise with the extra cost/inconvenience - "We are still worth the journey... but just incase you're in knots about the zone we're offering 'decongestion' juices for your pleasure!"

- Rents and/or business rates about to rise dramatically. In this case will you be able to pass on the new costs to your clients; will you need to change your market focus and move on to a more affluent group - if there is one in the area? Is this practical or realistic? If this is not possible you may need to start making plans to move your business! May be this will be the push you needed to get you to take the opportunity to move some of your money-making items *'off-land'* - meaning online! Either way, it is an absolute must that you revisit your figures (Step 3) and confirm exactly what effect this rent increase will have on your business.

- The business is in negative cash flow. Low cash flow is a serious threat and should be addressed as a matter of urgency. Once you have completed the necessary steps in this booklet to improving your revenues and reducing your costs, (you and) your business should go through a lean period during which you put all of your profits away thereby increasing your back-up funds to about 3-months worth of trading costs. If you're the sort that likes to treat yourself (and the team) after a period of *hard-work* then you are going to have to be content with a quite bottle of bubbly at home - this will not be the time for lavish pleasures!

- Another salon opening next door. This is only a threat if your offer is unclear and unattractive! See Step 7.

- Very high debts with some/all creditors - inland revenue, suppliers, landlord, etc. I think one of the biggest problems with this sort of threat is that it never seems to leave your mind and you find that you're just not able to do much else but worry and dwell! Understandably so, as your creditors indirectly have the power to close you down. If your business is worth saving - meaning it is a viable business but has just experienced unusual circumstances then I say do 4 things urgently :-

    1. Make sure you are not incurring any further debt. All creditors must be made aware of your position before you take on any more goods or services from them or anyone else.

    2. Write to all creditors explaining your situation, how it came about and your plan of action - after all some of them are in business too and need to know for their own cash flow!

    3. Prepare a document outlining a clear and strong plan of action attach this to

the Executive Summary of your business and start seeking a loan, investment or refinancing from your shareholders or other interested parties. Or use this document to try and negotiate longer payment terms with your creditors. Remember to add the SWOT to your executive summary, especially emphasising the strengths!

4. Maintain a constant eye on your cash flow; on a week by week basis!

The *Open Your Own Salon... The Right Way!* handbook covers in detail how to create an executive business summary and a meaningful profit & loss and cash flow forecast.

What are you doing to meet these threats head-on?

USING THIS INFORMATION

The SWOT will be different for different salons and situations, but doing a thorough analysis will give you a methodical way of working-out what is really great about your business, what isn't so great and where you may be missing out on crucial opportunities.

It will also help you prioritise where you need to focus your time and energy for maximum profit and long-term success.

It may be difficult, but be as objective about your business as possible; especially with its weaknesses. Imagine you are looking at another business and not your own. It's only through being thorough that you will give yourself the opportunity to improve or even eradicate the bad bits, while securing and growing the great bits!

STEP 2
STOP | START | CONTINUE

STOP

- Ignoring areas of your business that need your attention, both urgent and not urgent... don't wait for things to fall into the urgent category! Anything that's in your weaknesses and threats needs to be addressed now.
- Hoping that things will pick-up/get better/go away on their own; you must actively work on your business not just your clients.

START

- Focusing your energies on eliminating weaknesses and threats.
- Actively promoting and growing the strengths in your business.

CONTINUE

- To drive your business onwards and upwards!
- To enjoy your successes!

STEP 3
KNOW YOUR COSTS

LEARNING TO FOCUS ON COSTS AS WELL AS INCOME

When you're busy running a salon you may find that your focus is constantly on increasing revenue and not necessarily on controlling costs. You may think that the cost of running your business is just the by-product of your quest for more income - basically unavoidable and the best they can be. Following on from this, when times are hard and the business needs to rein in on costs there is a limited understanding on what costs to cut and what effect those cuts will have on income whether direct or indirect.

I recommend the following approach:-
Basically there are 3 actions you can take with regards to costs - Control | Reduce | Avoid

To start I would look at the costs of your last trading period (last year, last 6 months, last month, depending on how long you have been open) and try to package the outgoings under one of the above headings.

For example, below is a typical list of a salons costs:-

Stock; use and retail
Equipment maintenance
Staff
Rent and Business Rates
Management; admin and shopfloor
Licensing
Accounting
Heating, lighting, water
Bank Loan repayments
Bank charges and fines
Cleaning
Printing
Office supplies
Towels, robes
Telephone, Broadband
Shop alarm system

Beverages
Insurance (buildings, employer, public)
Marketing and PR
Training
Miscellaneous (repairs, underestimated costs, etc)

Here is the list again but sorted under Control | Reduce | Avoid

Control
Stock; use and retail
Equipment maintenance
Staff
Rent and Business Rates
Management; admin and shopfloor
Towels, robes
Telephone, Broadband
Beverages
Marketing and PR
Training
Licensing

I have placed the above list under Control as they all have a direct effect on customer service and should therefore show tangible returns to the business. Controlling, in this instance, also means 'keeping an eye on'.

- Staff wages will be your highest cost; especially if you are a salon that relies heavily on income earned from treatments. Control your wage bill by reviewing the productivity of your team members - is everyone pulling their weight? We will look into this more closely later in this Step and Step 4.
- Ensure that there is no wastage. For example are your marketing and training programmes yielding tangible returns; are the products being used correctly; breakage, spillage, theft under control; what about towel and phone usage.
- Try to stay on top of all your business costs at all times - know your costs - don't let them spiral out of control without you realising because you haven't got any mechanisms in place. Make sure you are regularly (at least monthly) maintaining a cash flow and profit & loss forecast. Immediately spot when expenditure has risen and income has not! *(For more assistance with this the 'Open Your Own Salon... The Right Way!' handbook has a chapter dedicated to creating and maintaining cash flow and profit & loss spreadsheets).*
- Understand what effect a rent or rates increase will have on your business. If there is such an increase check your prices to see if the business is still viable from that location.

Keep a limit on your costs.

Reduce

Stock - use only
Telephone, Broadband package
Accounting
Heating, lighting, water
Bank Loan repayments
Cleaning
Printing
Office supplies
Shop alarm system
Insurance (buildings, employer, public)

- Look at your utilities bills; could you be with a cheaper supplier? Check this on a price comparison website. Also you may be paying more than you need to by taking on a business tariff.
- Look at your supplier bills - Have you worked out how much the stock costs are per treatment? Are you using too many suppliers therefore not receiving the benefits of bulk ordering? Having said that, be sure to shop around for the best priced salon consumable items such as cotton, paper roll, couch roll, towels, buds, etc. These items can be some of the most costly, simply due to their continuous use.
- Save on accounting bills by providing organised expense and income records to your accountant.
- Use a recommended, individual accountant rather than a firm of accountants - firms can be costly.
- Review the prices you are paying for printing - there are many printing companies online offering great products and prices.
- Reduce your cleaning bill by maintaining a strict station maintenance policy and task rota; hire a cleaner only once a week to maintain the floors, furniture, walls and toilets and not to sort through stations and products.

Think about where else you can bring down the costs of running your business.

Avoid

Bank charges and fines
Inland Revenue fines
Miscellaneous (repairs, underestimated costs, etc)

- If you know you are about to go into debt or may be unable to meet a payment deadline be sure to contact the creditor in advance - this may be difficult but can help avoid fines and charges. Fines - late tax returns, unauthorised overdraft fees, court action, etc!

- Be prepared for the unexpected by making sure you have good insurance cover. Avoid the costs of accidents and repairs.

Think about what other costs you can prevent from happening.

WORKING-OUT COSTS AND PROFIT MARGINS FOR A SALON

Having looked at what actions can be taken with costs, let's look at an example salon - how much it costs to run it and how much money each treatment makes. Ideally you should follow the steps of this example inputting your salons actual figures.

But before all that ... a quick note about Goods Tax (VAT)

Remember if your business is registered for VAT then **whatever price you charge your clients for a treatment you are only really charging them that amount less goods tax**... This is easy to forget and often not accounted for by many!

Let's say goods tax is 15%.
So if you charge £10 for a manicure you are really charging 10 ÷ 1.15 = £8.70 for the manicure. This is a substantial 'cost' even if you are getting some back through purchases!

Example Salon

In this example I will assume a relatively affluent location and clientele. The salon is open 6 days a week, 8 hours a day and has 6 treatment stations (this is any area that generates income – spray tan booth, massage table, manicure desk, hairdresser chair, sunbed, etc.) All prices will include Goods Tax (VAT) at 15% and all costs will exclude Goods Tax.

I have estimated the following outgoings as being typical...

Stock

Depending on where you source your stock from, it usually costs around 12% of the overall revenue generated through treatments (except of course if you are a threading bar only!). Take a look at your past years trading and divide the total amount spent on stock by the total amount generated from treatments and multiply by 100... is it around 12%? *(Let me know what yours came to! Email me at ego@misssalon.com).*

Either way, note what it is as you will use this percentage in later calculations.

For the purpose of this example I will estimate the yearly sales of this business to be approximately £22,000 a month = £265k per year

Therefore the stock bill, at 12%, would be around £30,000 per year. About £26,000 less 15% Goods tax.

Wages

Let's estimate the wages of a technician/therapist/operator at £7.50 per hour. So with employers national insurance contributions this will be closer to £8/hr.

Therefore - fully staffed at all times the wages bill would be as follows:-

- ➔ per day = 6 staff x 8 hours x £8 per hour = £384 per day
- ➔ per week = £384 x 6 days a week = £2,304 per week
- ➔ **per year = £2,304 x 52 weeks = £119,808 per year**

Overheads

Rent and Business Rates £30,000
Management £25,000
Licensing £340
Accounting £600
Heating, lighting, water £1500
Bank Loan repayments £6000
Cleaning £500
Printing £400
Office supplies £160
Towels £300
Telephone, Broadband £600
Shop alarm system £400
Beverages £500
Insurance (buildings, employer, public) £700
Marketing and PR £2000
Training £1000
Miscellaneous (repairs, underestimated costs, etc) £1000

Total salon overheads per year £71,000

The Analysis

Total salon costs per year = £26,000 + £120,000 + £71,000 = £217,000

Salon sales = £265,000

Excluding VAT = £265,000 ÷ 1.15 = £230,400
Total costs = £217,000

Profit = £230,400 - £217,000 = £13,400
Profit Margin = (13,400 ÷ 230,400) x 100 = 5.8% This is really low!

Further analysis
In this particular example the salon is fully staffed with 6 stations manned at all times. How much then does each manned station generate per day?

(£265,000 ÷ 52weeks) ÷ 6 days ÷ 6 stations = £141.50 per manned station per day
This is pretty low and suggests that the same amount of turnover could be achieved with less people.

WORKING OUT PROFIT MARGINS ON INDIVIDUAL TREATMENTS

First we workout the overheads per station:
- ➔ per year = £71,000 ÷ 6 stations = £11,800 per year
- ➔ per week = £11,800 ÷ 52 weeks = £228.00 per week
- ➔ per day = £228 ÷ 6 days a week = £38.00 per day
- ➔ per hour = £38 ÷ 8 hours a day = £5 per hour

Example Treatments

Full Set of Nail Enhancements
Time – approximately 1 hour
Price - £50

Costs
Goods Tax or VAT (at 15%) = £6.50 [That is £50 ÷ 1.15 = £43.50, then £50 - £43.50=£6.50]
Technicians wages (including Employer NI Contributions) for 1 hour = £8
Stock used at 12% of price = £6 (£50 × 12%)
Overheads for 1 hour = £5

Total Costs = £25.50
Gross Profit = £24.50
Gross Profit margin = 49% [That is (£24.50 (profit) ÷ £50 (price)) × 100]

Eyebrow and Forehead Threading
Time - approximately 10 minutes
Price - £20

Costs
Goods Tax or VAT (at 15%) = £2.60
Technicians wages for 10 minutes = £1.30
Cost of stock used = £0 (a string of thread)
Overheads = £0.80

Total Costs = £4.70
Gross Profit = £15.30
Gross Profit margin = 76% wow! [That is (15.30 ÷ 20) × 100]

Facial
Time - approximately 1 hour
Price - £55

Costs
Goods Tax or VAT (at 15%) = £7.20
Technicians wages for 1 hour = £8
Cost of stock used = £6.60
Overheads = £5

Total Costs = £26.70
Gross Profit = £28.30
Gross Profit margin = 51% [That is (28.30 ÷ 55) × 100]

Spray Tan
Time - approximately 15 minutes
Price - £20

Costs
Goods Tax or VAT (at 15%) = £2.60
Technicians wages for 15 minutes = £2
Cost of stock used = £2.40
Overheads = £1.25

Total Costs = £8.25
Gross Profit = £11.75
Gross Profit margin = 58% [That is (11.75 ÷ 20) × 100]

As you can see, some treatments are obviously more profitable than others. The point of this exercise is to highlight the key factors that make the difference – the time taken to provide the treatment and therefore the staff wages, the amount of product used during the treatment and your overheads.

From this example we see that for every hour a station is staffed but not in use, without a client, costs the business £13 (£5 in overheads + £8 in wages). For every hour a station is not staffed, costs the business £5. This means that after 2 hours of no activity all the profits made from a full set of nail enhancements are gone!

So if one was to try and implement a cost cutting exercise without giving it proper consideration, you might think of:-

1. Letting some of your staff go – but then who will perform the treatments;
2. Getting your staff to work faster – but what difference would that make if the next customer isn't waiting and what would happen to the customer experience?
3. Looking for cheaper supplies – this would definitely be a sensible move as long as it didn't affect the quality of the treatments;
4. Reducing the business overheads – another sensible move but which ones?
5. Reduce your rent bill – easier said than done; just moving could blow the budget! You could, however, try renegotiating your terms with your landlord; you never know!

The point is that if a cost cutting exercise is the emergency action you need to take to keep your salon doors open then I suggest a methodical and planned approach to deciding and implementing those cuts. (See Good cost / Bad cost on page 28)

Do all of the above for your salon, using real figures, and then make decisions based on what's in front of you in black and white.

Here is another way of looking at overheads:-

Overhead	Per Year	Per Month	Per Week	Per Day
Rent and Business Rates	£30,000.00	£2,500.00	£576.92	£96.15
Management	£25,000.00	£2,083.33	£480.77	£80.13
Bank Loan repayments	£6,000.00	£500.00	£115.38	£19.23
Heating, lighting, water	£1,500.00	£125.00	£28.85	£4.81
Marketing and PR	£2,000.00	£166.67	£38.46	£6.41
Training	£1,000.00	£83.33	£19.23	£3.21
Licensing	£340.00	£28.33	£6.54	£1.09
Accounting	£600.00	£50.00	£11.54	£1.92
Cleaning	£500.00	£41.67	£9.62	£1.60
Printing	£400.00	£33.33	£7.69	£1.28
Office supplies	£160.00	£13.33	£3.08	£0.51
Towels	£300.00	£25.00	£5.77	£0.96

Overhead	Per Year	Per Month	Per Week	Per Day
Telephone, Broadband	£600.00	£50.00	£11.54	£1.92
Shop alarm system	£400.00	£33.33	£7.69	£1.28
Beverages	£500.00	£41.67	£9.62	£1.60
Insurance (buildings, employer, public)	£700.00	£58.33	£13.46	£2.24
Miscellaneous (repairs, underestimated costs, etc)	£1,000.00	£83.33	£19.23	£3.21
TOTAL	**£71,000.00**	**£5,916.67**	**£1,365.38**	**£227.56**

So... approximately £230 a day in overheads alone... *This can really give you something to think about!* I personally would make a decision at this stage to aim to retail a minimum of £250 per day and cover at least half of overheads.

IN CONCLUSION...

By doing this sort of analysis you make the business costs known, tangible and therefore controllable.

You empower yourself to...

- Make informed decisions on what discounts you can give your customers.
- Understand how productive individual team members are being in terms of treatment timings.
- Decide which costs are 'good' and which ones are 'bad'; Good costs are ones that produce what customers want and are willing to pay for - these costs have tangible returns. Bad costs are those that do not produce any beneficial or tangible returns to the business because they add nothing to what your customers are willing to pay for. Bad costs are the ones that should be avoided or reduced! So for example, spending on training your team to do nail art for a market that predominately consists of natural-nail types would be a waste of money and therefore a bad cost. Merchandising your salon and trying to retail expensive face cleansers and creams in a market that can't afford or even worse, don't see the point of this product, is also a waste of money and therefore a bad cost. Printing price lists on 300gsm card instead of 250gsm card, and paying more for this, when it makes no difference to your clients expectations is also a waste of money.

Spend your money creating the environment and providing the items and treatments your customers want and value as 'discovered' in step 1.

STEP 3
STOP | START | CONTINUE

STOP

- Ignoring your costs
- Any wastage and haemorrhaging of money through neglect and poor money management... needless to say, this is ***crucial***! However how would you know if you don't take a look...?

START

- Maintaining and monitoring a regular cash flow and profit & loss forecast - therefore knowing and understanding your costs
- Controlling, reducing and avoiding 'bad' costs
- Investing money into 'good' costs

CONTINUE

- To drive your business onwards and upwards!
- To enjoy your successes!

STEP 4 ASSESS YOUR TEAM & REVIEW YOUR MANAGEMENT STYLE

ASSESSING YOUR TEAM

Why bother assessing your team? You may think you already know 'your lot' pretty well - after all you hired them and may be working with them everyday. But what you know about them may not be the whole picture - besides what is really important is what your customers think of the service they provide and what they, your employee, thinks of their job!

And then there's the friend/boss issue - if there isn't a clear line drawn you may have found yourself in a situation were you are unable to reprimand without it being taken personally or worse you may have become so involved in their private life that you can't be objective about them as a productive member of the team!

Whatever the case may be your salon employees are everything to your business - in most cases they are the main revenue generators as well as your highest cost... and they are also human beings! So officially assessing your team and using your findings to make the necessary corrections in the proper way will go a long way towards increasing your bottom line and your sanity!

Assessing your team entails the following checks:-

- Quality of the treatments they provide
- Quality of the customer service they give
- The speed and efficiency of their service
- That their needs are being met - they are happy in their job, feel valued and inspired to give their best on a day-to-day basis.

- ***The quality of the treatments - assessing actual skill levels***

First things first, what is the true quality of the treatments provided in your salon? The only way to honestly answer this question is through a series of mystery shopper reports. As demonstrated in Step 3, the cost of this *invaluable* exercise would be the cost of all the treatments the mystery shoppers have, that is, the spray-tan at £8.25 or the facial at £26.70. Most mystery shoppers would be happy to come in a have the treatment for free in return for a full report on their experience and whether or not they would come again and actually spend the money...!

One thing I have definitely come across in abundance is 'OK' treatments... nothing really wrong but nothing really right either. Hair cut but the wash was not that good; spray tan but the result is a bit patchy the next day; pedicure but the nails are shaped a bit crooked; eyebrows shaped but not really even; massage but not enough pressure; salt scrub but whole sections missed, waxing but stray hairs not removed... these sorts of errors are never 'serious' enough for a client to make a complaint; ***instead they just don't come back***, and you will be left thinking everything is fine with your offer it's just the client who isn't a salon junkie! How many one-off visits have you had to your shop? Why not look through your client records and see what percentage of people have only visited once; if it's more than 50% I would say you need to start looking for a pattern.

"Even bad customer service is tolerated when results are excellent"

If you have been a salon owner for a while you would no doubt have experienced that girl who just keeps on getting repeat bookings; her column is always packed. Then there's the girl who is always available for the walk-in client, mostly because her column is not full. Unfortunately her column is not full because she is not doing a good job... and handing over these ***precious*** walk-in's, ie. new business, to her is actually damaging your business! They come in for a treatment - having made the decision to trust your salon, having been enticed by whatever marketing you have done - only to be semi disappointed or just left feeling neither here nor there about their experience... *WHAT A WASTE!*

The truth is that nobody has on-going money for 'OK'; they will continue to take their cash to someone else until they finally find excellent! Interestingly even good customer service can't save a series of 'OK' treatments but even more interestingly, bad customer service is tolerated when results are excellent!

So back to solution mode... organise a series of mystery shoppers to visit your salon; provide them with a form to complete after their visit helping you make a proper assessment of your salons services. Remember to ask the all important question - Would you come back and pay to have this treatment again - with us, with the same therapist? Remember you are aiming for excellent!

If you're getting bad news, or if you already know who is not doing such a good job, then take action immediately. Handle poor performance by putting that staff member on a time-bound Performance Review Programme and providing immediate training or re-training... it's really the only way to give that person an opportunity to improve and if not, to fairly dismiss them.

Where can I find mystery shoppers?

Anyone can be a mystery shopper, however you would ideally like to find someone who represents your core market and is articulate enough to convey their experience accurately in writing. Miss Salon provide mystery shoppers *(currently UK only)*. The advantage of using us is that even you will not know when they will visit or who they are, hence making it even more objective. Our mystery shoppers will complete our prepared questionnaire after leaving your establishment which will be sent directly to you; this is completely confidential and Miss Salon do not keep any record of their report. We charge a £20 admin fee per visit. Book one or more today 0845 643 1619. *(Prices may vary)*

- ***The quality of the customer service provided***

What is required to provide exceptional customer service?

Exceptional customer service comes from within... it's just not one of those superficial, forced things. If your staff member is not focused on their job, but rather on some other social interest (for example) and they do not value the job they do, the quality of the customer service they provide will inevitably be average or poor.

To provide exceptional customer service the following is required:-

1. Pride in ones work and the work place environment
2. The ability to focus on the day ahead and therefore focus on the clients *(see ideas of how to create this below in Daily Management)*
3. A desire to serve and to be of service
4. Value the job

Again, use mystery shoppers to gain a customers view on how good your service is. If you could be doing better, speak to your team, individually and as a group, and investigate the 4 areas listed above.

A note about point 3 - A desire to serve and to be of service - I would like to comment on this point in particular because I have seen first hand what a lack of this character trait can do to in this industry. I think that any beauty therapist, nail technician, hairdresser or any other kind of beauty & wellbeing professional that does not realise that they are in the business of serving an individual's personal needs is in the wrong business.

Customer service and your brand

Your team are your first brand ambassadors - they promote, advertise and create the service and experience - what they do defines your salon in the mind of the client. For example, Citibank, Sainsbury's or Hilton Hotels could spend millions of dollars on advertising campaigns and marketing material but the way their customer-facing staff treat you at the counter, check-out or reception desk will create a lasting impression in your mind about the brand.

Train your team to understand the impact they have on your brand. Help them understand that being good brand ambassadors is part of their job description. ***Show them*** how to do a good job through role play, rehearsals and practice.

- ***Checking speed and efficiency***

Checking the speed and efficiency of your team is all about keeping your profit margins in check. As shown in Step 3, if individuals take longer or misuse product during a treatment this can have cost implications and therefore affect your bottom-line.

Create regular training and practice sessions helping to eliminate waste and increase quality and speed.

- ***Are they happy at work?***

Well, needless-to-say, if they are not happy at work they are not going to do a good job. Even the best of them, with strong work ethics, will falter under the pressure of disliking some aspect of their job. It may not be the job that's the problem; they could be unhappy about some other aspect of their life.

I know you are not in the business of life coaching or counselling and you don't want to cross the line between boss and friend but taking a little interest and providing a listening ear to some of their woes can increase trust and good feelings which makes management easier and can increase motivation.

I would also like to point out in this section that in general I have found that one of the main reasons people become beauty professionals is the fact that they get instant job satisfaction when a client is happy - it's 'good vibe' work - so having said that if the salon as a whole has a great reputation amongst its customers; they love the treatments, customer service and environment - this in turn increases staff 'happiness' and therefore productivity.

So what did you find out?

Is customer service excellent; treatment quality worth paying for, worth coming back for? Are the therapists keeping to time and using products efficiently therefore maintaining or increasing your profit margins? Do they value their job? Do they feel valued at work? Are they smiling!?

REVIEWING YOUR MANAGEMENT STYLE

Now some of you may be great managers but most are not! Sorry, but it's true. Being a good manager and leader of people whilst running a business as well requires a diverse set of skills and character attributes. Nobody's perfect but we can all aim to do a better job. In this section I will attempt to touch on some of the main issues with management that could directly affect your profits, however if you are *seriously* struggling to manage your team then you should consider getting some people management training.

So I will discuss the following:-

- Where are you?
- Daily management tools & methods

Where are you - are you in the treatment rooms or running your business?

So firstly, I think it is safe to say that if you are the only manager of your staffed salon then it is impossible to effectively run your business as well as service a full list of appointments.

I think it is also safe to say that if you are only managing the admin side of your salon and don't know 'much' about what goes on in the treatment rooms or on your money-making stations then that's a serious problem as well. Now I'm not saying that you should be able to jump-in and take-over if a treatment needs doing (or saving!) but you must have a good understanding of the processes involved, therefore the correct product and equipment usage and the expected results. If this is you, get some training, watch some demos, have the treatments done yourself.

If you are guilty of the former then you must, absolutely must, reduce the number of hours you work on clients and dedicate at least 60% of your working week to running the business. If you don't you will run yourself ragged trying to keep up with all the demands on your time; from staff, to clients, to paperwork, and end up not doing any of it well and just making yourself unwell! If you have clients who just categorically refuse, no matter what you offer them, to go to another operator then they will either need to fit into your new treatment hours or go away! Now I am not one to ever advocate letting ***any*** clients go, but ultimately this business was started so that you could make money, working for yourself and doing what you love. If that has turned into you having to put your dreams on-hold because there aren't enough hours in the day and Ms Smith won't budge then Ms Smith needs to go! Hopefully what you will find, as you spend more time steering your ship in the right direction and creating more growth opportunities, is that more clients will get to know about and experience the benefits of your establishment.

Achieving this requires that you make the time to find them, attract them and meet their expectations so that the business can grow.

Daily Management Tools & Methods

In this section I will briefly address a variety of daily staff management issues and methods:-

Creating focus

- **Sales targets**

Setting daily sales targets can be a very effective method of getting your team to focus on the day ahead. If your salon is situated in a high foot-fall area then setting sales targets can help motivate the team to attract more customers or perform treatments in a timely manner so as to be free for the next walk-in. Sale targets also keep staff focused on retailing products - if they are smart, and lucky, they could hit their target for the day with the first client!

Set your daily sales targets from your P&L (profit and loss). For example:-
Say your P&L forecasts a turnover of £265k in a year then...
£265,000/52 weeks = £5,100 per week
£5,100/6 trading days = **£850 per day**

£850/4 staff = £215 per staff per day

- **Give sales targets meaning...**

If it helps why not turn the £215 into something more tangible, for example:-
3 facials at £55 each
3 face creams at £17.50 each
This gives the therapists even more of a focus; anything on top of that will be a bonus!

- **Incentives and creating a competitive yet friendly environment**

Offering your staff incentives for great performance is an excellent way of officially rewarding hard work. Cash bonuses, vouchers and holidays are great, but whatever you do make sure you set up a clear, fair and achievable incentive scheme.

Healthy competition within the team also goes a long way towards maintaining a team spirit, whilst keeping them focused and motivated; ultimately driving sales!

- **Daily Station-Start | Station-End checks**

An additional method for creating focus and running an organised salon is to create daily station checks. Make individuals responsible for maintaining pristine and fully stocked stations, ready for their next clients.

On-going monitoring & motivating

Keep a check on all your processes by organising regular:-

- staff performance reviews
- in-house salon inspections
- mystery shopper visits

Keep your team informed through regular:-

- staff meetings
- open discussions

Keep your team empowered through:-

- clear written processes
- written and understood company policies
- training and rehearsal

Keep your team motivated and working as a team through:-

- group incentives (the teams effort wins)
- cash bonuses, popular store vouchers and prizes
- days/nights out

- **Training and rehearsals**

Keep your team performing at their best by raising self-esteem through regular in-house training and rehearsals sessions. The service you provide should be 'effortless perfection'; this can only be achieved through training and rehearsal! Role play in the salon; give everyone the opportunity to walk through different scenarios, perform treatments and close product sales. Make it fun, friendly and interesting. Make sure everyone has bought into the process and understands the need for this... Sorry to be cheesy but think "wax on, wax off"...

Do these rehearsals together again and again and again until you achieve effortless perfection.

- **Motivating the team during quite periods**

Quite periods can be a spirit killer... well, they are just *sooo* boring! The team can easily go down hill during these times; gossip, idleness, stress due to potentially reduced earnings... by the time a client walks in, the desire to serve and the focus on service is gone. I'm sure you've experienced this before on one of those 'quite floors' in a department store - you approach the counter to ask a question, two sales assistants are *very busy* chatting and your presence is treated as a nuisance! You see, they have become very use to their world in the shop and they have certain expectations of their working day like, catching-up with the gossip from Sally's night-out, sorting out the car insurance, checking on friends through facebook, planning lunch and dinner or discussing the very important purchase issue of the Chloe handbag that's just arrived in store! It is the kind of behaviour that were it witnessed by the store owner or senior management they would be horrified. But these employees can't be given all the blame; they are bored and the mind looks for distractions.

The only way to prevent this from happening in your salon is to create a task rota. At any one time there are loads of things to do in a salon - refilling nail tip boxes, shampoo pumps and other station products, checking testers, buffing display shelves and sorting through client records. But rather than conjure up tasks to fill in time - which suggests that the tasks are not really that important and that you are just looking for a way to make 'them work' - create a task rota.

Task rota pros:-

- Great way of fairly and thoroughly allocating important salon tasks to all the team.
- Makes individuals responsible for things that benefit the team and the business.
- The tasks can be rotated week-by-week.
- Prevents the need for you to randomly conjure up work - especially when you may already be in an irritated mood
- Provides 'important' work for individuals to do even when you are not around and they don't have a booking.

Remember tasks can include marketing activity - leafleting, talking to passers-by about the services, offering treatment samples and product testers.

Whatever happens make sure your team know what to do to keep busy, whether they have bookings or not, whether you are in the salon or not.

- **Don't forget the simple things...**

Acknowledging a job well done in an honest way shows you value your teams efforts and appreciate good work. Even if you think that "it's their job; why should you praise them just for getting-on with it"... Well let's put it this way - a parent's job, for example, is to make sure that their child is fed but a thank you from that child every so often goes a long way to making mum and dad feel appreciated.

*So remember to **smile** and say **thank you**... no matter how stressed you are about business!*

ONE BAD APPLE

Employees who 'sit in the boat but don't pull the oars' take their toll on the rest of the team and are therefore a liability to your business. Not pulling the oars includes incompetence, antisocial behaviour (gossiping, excluding, being rude or intimidating), laziness, tardiness and showing no regard for salon rules such as timekeeping, cleaning, attending staff meetings and so on. Unfortunately they are far more toxic than you can imagine and have the power to ruin the team dynamic, causing an array of never-ending problems. It is best to realise that these people and the issues they create generally only get worse and you must address and deal with them fast.

If the individual is within their initial probation period of the job then I wouldn't hesitate to let them go... pronto. If they are bad at the start they will only get worse, simple.

Otherwise, I suggest a relaxed 'chat' off the shop floor to try and establish the root cause of any problems they may be having. Find out if there is some way you can help them be more productive and positive within the business in the short-term? Look for a quick win. If this is not possible then you should put them on a time-bound performance improvement programme (performance review followed by a course of action) and/or the disciplinary process.

Importantly, remember that these things don't just get better on their own and sometimes there is no amount of 'talking' that will correct the problem, hence it is very important to formalise your 'chats' so that they become part of your process - this way you can get rid of repeat offenders with a record of your 'warnings' and attempts to help them improve.

SUMMARY

Reduce many of your worst management tasks by creating consistent policies and processes. Save yourself the drama of having to make things up as you go along or having to constantly be there to see the place run smoothly. Empower your team to get on with their jobs effectively and efficiently by creating:-

- Training and rehearsal days
- Performance review programme
- Task rota
- A customer complaint policy and procedure
- Disciplinary procedure
- Salon operations manual

- A staff handbook
- Health & Safety policy and procedures manual

See www.misssalon.com for an array of various salon documents designed to make managing your business easier.

STEP 4
STOP | START | CONTINUE

STOP

- Expecting excellence if no time is spent developing your people.
- Running yourself into the ground because you haven't motivated and empowered your team to work hard and know how things work in your salon.
- Ignoring 'toxic' employees

START

- Incorporating clear and written processes and procedures for the team
- Regular mystery shopper visits
- Training and rehearsal days
- Regular and formal performance reviews
- Including your team in decision making
- Ensuring that everyone knows and understands the businesses strategy statement

CONTINUE

- To drive your business onwards and upwards!
- To enjoy your successes!

STEP 5 CHECK YOUR RECEPTION DESK & BOOKING PROCESS

If you are already in business then you must be in no doubt as to the importance of this area / salon function. If you started your salon thinking the reception desk was nothing more than a table for the till then by now you would have had a rude awakening!

Next to the administration office of your business, the reception desk is the customer facing, centre of organisation of your salons day-to-day operations. But remember, this booklet is less about operations and more about key actions to profitability; so I won't talk about how to setup and run your reception functions but more about how to keep your till ringing! For more on reception setup and a more detailed look at all salon operations, please read the *'Open Your Own Salon... The Right Way!'* handbook.

"The reception desk is the customer facing, centre of organisation of your salons day-to-day operations"

TURN YOUR RECEPTION DESK INTO A MONEY-MAKING STATION

Just as your treatment rooms and hair stations are money-making stations, so too should your reception desk be. I even think it's not a bad idea to create sales targets for the reception desk/receptionist!

Have you noticed how your local corner shop always has a ton of items right next to the till... well that's because in that location, the pay point, you're very likely to be tempted to buy more than you'd planned. You may have popped in for a tin of beans and some milk, but you'll probably leave with an extra packet of crisps and some gum... because they were staring at you, right!

Do the same for your reception desk - source well chosen items, items that appeal to your target market, to place by the till and watch them fly off with almost every client. Keep in mind when choosing what items to sell at reception, that price is crucial here - items must be less than £10, preferably £5 - they should be low involvement/commitment for the buyer. If they are not shifting then they are wrong for that area, so try something else. Be dynamic about this; things are not suppose to stay collecting dust in your salon - they are suppose to sell.

Read more about successful merchandising and retailing of products in Step 8.

THE RECEPTIONIST - SALON COORDINATOR

A skilled receptionist is key in the quest for profit. They are the first and last person a customer sees and hears. Not only are they a major part of the first-impression, but they are also in charge of your appointment system - bookings, reminders, cancellations, staff lunches & breaks, payments and sales logs. When the salon is busy (which is the aim), the receptionist can be the only person available to clients... The receptionist:-

- Represents your salon
- Runs the appointment system, including staff lunches and breaks
- Sees to waiting clients
- Closes sales and seeks opportunities to recommend additional services and products
- Answers questions about treatments and products
- May be first to handle a customer complaint
- Must know how long individual therapists/techs take to complete treatments
- Reports on the days sales to the team and management
- Is faced with satisfied and dissatisfied customers
- Needs to be friendly, efficient, knowledgeable, well-presented, articulate and a natural sales person

Think about the *maitre d'* at a restaurant - this is the person who overseas the restaurant front-of-house and handles reservations; they are not necessarily the restaurant manager or owner.

The INTANGIBLE benefits of a good maitre d' from a customers perspective...

A good maitre d' knows all the regulars by name, ensures that they are welcomed and seen to in the right way; he highlights items on the menu that may be of interest and answers any questions customers may have. A *excellent* maitre d' senses the occasion and provides the intangible extras that make the visit all the more memorable. When you call to make a booking he will do all he can to fit you in and give you a sense that an effort has been made and your needs are going to be met.

The TANGIBLE benefits from the businesses perspective...

- Customers are relaxed and ready for the service.
- Extra dishes are sold due to recommendation from the maitre d' who has gained the trust of the customer.
- Advance bookings are made.
- Restaurant floor staff are managed and assisted throughout.
- A 'person-ality' has been given to the restaurant therefore a sense of loyalty or human connection has been made with the restaurant.

All of these things apply to a salon. The receptionist should be like the maitre d'; coordinating the activities in the salon between clients, techs and treatments.

Rather than Receptionist, I think the title 'Salon Coordinator' is a more appropriate for this job; it seems to better define the responsibilities and expectations associated with the role. I realise that skilled and experienced people come at a price and you will need to balance the cost of their wages against the benefit of having them on the shop floor, but don't see this as a financial waste of time. If your salon is in a high or average footfall area then I would highly recommend hiring a skilled coordinator and investing the money; they should play a big role in getting clients in, booked and spending with you. If you are in a low footfall area then I would search for someone who would be prepared to work on a basic plus commission basis; say earning commission for every booking, re-booking and reception area sale.

Top tip for finding the best salon coordinators

Search for a sales person, someone who has worked in sales not someone who was, is or hopes to be a therapist, hairdresser, etc. They need to have the finesse and looks that are attractive in a salon and should be beauty enthusiasts. In the past I have found the best ones to be beauty department store girls, like the ones who have worked on cosmetic counters such as Benefit, MAC, Clarins etc. The most dynamic of these people are a major asset to a salon - they have been trained in selling techniques, they understand sales targets, beauty products and the customer mind-set. They are also merchandising experts and have experience in creating effective seasonal marketing displays.

Visit a department store and ask the makeup counter girls what websites, publications and agencies they use when they are looking for work. Advertise for your salon coordinator there! Try to find out what they earn; some may be willing to share their salary information with you (this is important - you must know what the going rate is and consider your business needs in return). You will be surprised that these girls don't cost as much as you may think and the right one will bring a whole new dynamic into your salon. Whatever you do, do not leave this job to a shy or worse, bored young girl who just wants to get home!

CRUCIAL BOOKING PROCESS DO'S & DON'TS

Can't fit client in at preferred time | fully booked

How many times have I called a salon to make an appointment and with not so much as a pleasant sigh the receptionist tells me there is no availability at the time I want... just a brief "Sorry, Laurain's fully booked tomorrow"... with a tone that says, the ball is now in your court you can say bye-bye and go or ask me another question.

The problem with this is... from the customers point-of-view the ***salon*** is basically saying - Sorry but we have so many clients, we don't really need your business, you're not following our rules and booking well in advance, you are actually distracting us from our many other clients, ask another question and we *might* be able to help you otherwise we can afford to not keep/seek your business.

Instead... I suggest a more appreciative-of-your-business and therefore helpful response like:-

Client - "Hello, it's Sylvia Wedlock speaking, I'd like to book an appointment for tomorrow with Laurain for a wash and style please."

Receptionist - "Hello Sylvia, nice to hear from you again... Let me have a look for you... well it *looks like* Laurain is fully booked tomorrow - is there any other time/day that would suit you?"

Client - "No, I have a last minute event to attend, I urgently need my hair done tomorrow."

Receptionist - "Oh wow, I see, well I have another *absolutely excellent* hairdresser who can do your hair tomorrow. She has been with us for many years/months and has a really loyal client base... our clients love her. Would you like me to book you in with her?

Client - "She sounds great, but if there is anyway I can have Laurain I would rather stick with her."

Receptionist - "Ok, let me see what I can do and call you back within the hour; in the meantime I will pencil you in with Paula to secure your space"

Even if there isn't much you can do... at least make a an effort to try to help!

Remember your main 'product' are the treatments! Can you imagine what would happen if I walked into a supermarket wanting to buy a carton of milk, when I get to the shelf that usually stocks milk, I find it empty, but behind the sales desk are 100 cartons of milk waiting to be placed on the shelf. I say, can I have a carton of milk please, and the sales girl says sorry madam we are out of stock, the shelves are empty. But there's loads of milk behind you. Yes, but they're not out on the shelf yet...

That's just unhelpful!

She is saying don't want your money, don't value your custom, we can sell this milk with or without you, don't care, go away.

Think of your treatments as products - you cannot turn willing, wanting, dialing-your-salon-number clients away without doing your very best to fit them in and see that they are offered alternatives that are relevant to their needs.

"Never let them go... always see what you can do"

"...remember this person dialed ***YOUR*** number or walked into ***YOUR*** salon... isn't that the point of ***ALL*** the marketing you do... isn't that the point of your salon!??"

Appointment reminders & availability

Remember this booklet is about profit, so I won't discuss the different methods of reminding clients of their appointments rather the fact that reminders are a must. Reminders work both ways; they remind a client of their booking (this is particularly nice if you have a cancellation fee) and they also give you advance notice incase they are unable to show, saving you turning others away.

Many salons have already adapted to the latest technology and have automatic appointment reminders sent out to clients via mobiles and internet. These are great as customers can update their virtual diaries on the go. Still many people and salons are using paper diaries and use appointment reminder cards instead - this is fine too.

Another really good reception function is to send out text messages to clients when there is 'unexpected' availability. Obviously you want to keep a check on how many times you contact a client unsolicited, including the regular offers you make them aware of, so don't go overboard. However, sending the occasional text to a client saying... Hello Sylvia, just wanted to let you know that Laurain is available for a blow-dry today at 4, would you like to take that booking? Or Hi Rachel, fancy a manicure - your favourite manicurist Anita is free at 2 tomorrow. Should I book you in?... is not a bad thing.

Once you've tried a few of these, see how they are working and ask you clients whether they appreciate receiving these texts? I am sure that most won't mind, especially if they are not expected to respond when not interested and also especially if they love the service they get with you.

*These sort of texts, using simple **friendly** language, can be perceived as nice reminders to take some unexpected 'me-time'... whilst filling appointment gaps and increasing revenue!*

A cancellation fee

This is particularly important if you are a busy salon or in a high footfall area. You cannot afford to continue to lose income through no-shows or last minute cancellations. Having said that if you have one of those super salon coordinators I spoke about earlier, she/he would be on top of all the appointment activity and would rarely not be able to fit someone in!... yes this is possible in a busy salon! (I had a girl like that in one of my busiest salons; she was fantastic - knew all the regulars, was welcoming to all the new clients, sold a ton of products, organised the girls; she was fast, sharp and active - a real asset).

Anyway, if it isn't possible to charge a cancellation fee then I suggest a robust process of contacting your clients 48/24 hours in advance of any appointment to make sure you cut down the likelihood of a no-show.

Party bookings

These can be tricky and need skill and time taken to understand the needs of the client. I recommend that rather than trying to do all the bookings over the phone or in person, there and then you should setup a process for handling bookings of 4 or more people.

May be something like this:-

- Provide the customer with the treatment menu/pricelist - either email, download from website or hand over in person if they visit the shop.
- Proceed with the process of assisting them decide on what treatments they would like. Hopefully you have a menu that is self-explanatory but if not then you will need to set aside at least 10/15 minutes to discuss their needs and expectations of the day; helping them choose the right treatments.
- Once complete, take this information away and without keeping them on hold or standing around in the shop while you understand who can do what and when, tell the client you will get back to them by the next day with their schedule of treats!

This way you can keep your behind the scenes drama out of sight plus you can discuss how you can increase the value of their day and money in your till through additional treatments and services (like if you have the space, providing food, champagne, decorations, etc)

Party bookings are great and can make the business a lot of money in one go plus bring in new clients that should be converted into regulars!

Re-booking

There is a skill to re-booking clients before they leave the salon. Simply asking "Would you like to book your next appointment now?" Is mostly answered with a "No". This could be for a number of reasons:-

1. They were not overly impressed with the treatment they just had or the salon as a whole
2. They can't make the financial commitment to another treatment
3. They can't make the time commitment to another treatment
4. They can't think that far ahead and don't see that treatment as crucial to their daily life
5. They don't see the benefit of booking in advance; they have always been seen to in the past and there are no other incentives for early booking

By identifying the most common reasons for not wanting to re-book in your salon, you can create ways to address these 'hidden' concerns. For example, 2,3 and 5 could be addressed by offering an attractive discount for any booking made straight after a treatment. 4 could be addressed by highlighting the benefits (or the importance) of maintaining a treatment programme - so for example, a full-set of nails must be in-filled regularly to maintain their look; book your next visit now and get 10% off your infill. If however the reason is 1, then how you handle it falls into your customer complaints policy.

In all of these do think about a cancellation fee or a process that contacts clients well in advance of the appointment to keep any potential revenue losses in check.

STEP 5
STOP | START | CONTINUE

STOP

- Ignoring crucial revenue streams
- Underestimating the importance of your receptionist and reception area
- Hiring inadequate and unenthusiastic reception staff

START

- Retailing more from your reception area/desk
- Expecting more from your receptionist/salon coordinator - this powerful job is for someone from a beauty sales background
- Expecting to pay more for a great salon coordinator
- Enthusiastically welcoming clients into the salon
- Converting telephone and walk-in enquiries into actual bookings

CONTINUE

- To search for the right person to run your front-of-house; don't settle for mediocre.
- To drive your business onwards and upwards!
- To enjoy your successes!

STEP 6
IS THE STAGE SET - CAN THE SHOW BEGIN?

STAGE... WHAT STAGE?

What stage?? Your salon stage! Your salon is a stage! There is a set, actors and customers who come to enjoy the daily performance... In order for the show to run smoothly, day in day out, everything needs to be ready...

The Set - clean, organised and designed to create the right backdrop to your salons 'show'.

The Actors (in costume) - trained, experienced and rehearsed ready to perform with the same high standard again and again.

Think of your salon business as a show, with no room for shop floor errors and visible behind the scene operations - this is how all successful businesses are presented.

WHAT DOES YOUR SALON LOOK LIKE?

Your shop front and the salon itself is the first connection you make with clients. Remember you are in the business of grooming and beautifying and as such you must ensure that your salon plays its part in making clients feel that they are in the right place!

What does your salon look like? Is it the lovely neat, clean, efficient and welcoming place you dreamt of at the start or has it turned into a mess of mismatched furniture, cluttered work stations, grubby corners, messy shelves, dusty museum-like displays, broken signs and equipment, unused areas, stained walls, piles of old magazines and an untidy reception desk? I know the salon is your baby and nobody wants to be told their baby is ugly... but sometimes we are so caught-up in the day-to-day that we stop seeing the salon the way others do; especially new potential customers. So take off your emotional, nostalgic glasses and take a really good objective look at your salons' interior and exterior and make two lists: the good and the bad! What works for your business and what's got to go! To be sure that your are being as objective as possible you should enlist the input of your staff, friends and family – please pick people who are not just going to be 'nice' to you. At the end of the day, this is your business we are talking about and its survival, so lets get real.

IS YOUR SALON CLEAN?

Of course this would be the cheapest of all problems to have as all that's required is a proper spring clean! If you are closed one day in the week then that's the day to do your salon wash-down; if not then I'm afraid you are going to have to do what all 7-day a week shops do and that is an all-nighter!

You might think that polishing the taps or having spotless walls is not that big a deal and won't make much of a difference but that's just not true... it's the difference between having properly shaped eyebrows or not! A person who's had their eyebrows freshly shaped or their hair freshly relaxed has a certain 'bright' look about them you can't quite pinpoint. This is the same for your shop.

Get behind, through and around everything – move the furniture, remove all the posters and stickers and framed certificates, paint your walls, buff the floors, change the containers, change the towels, have any unsightly holes, gaps, mould repaired, dust all the shelves, de-clutter and polish all the surfaces. Where possible repair or replace broken equipment and furniture.

Once everything has been cleaned and repaired be mindful of what you put back... don't just stick the old posters and put all the old bits and pieces back... think about whether they still look good or have any relevance to your market. Do your customers come to your shop because of these things? Just try and think that less is more and the less 'junk' you have on your walls, windows and in your shop the better!

Monitor the state of your salon and maintain this cleaning through regular salon inspections and a task rota.

But one thing's for sure though... the show cannot begin without stocked and organised work stations. Ensuring a daily Station-Start/Station-End check keeps your money-makers, the stations, ready for action!

STEP 6
STOP | START | CONTINUE

STOP
- Sticking posters on the salon walls and windows willy-nilly
- Adding bits of furniture from all over
- Hoarding old magazines
- Ignoring broken furniture, equipment, signage

START
- Having things repaired as soon as needed
- Cleaning the salon on a daily basis
- Having the shop front exterior cleaned regularly
- Organising your work stations every day

CONTINUE
- To take pride in your salon and how you present it to the world

STEP 7 ATTRACTING CUSTOMERS - CREATING BRAND AMBASSADORS

MARKETING

First things first, what is Marketing? Put simply, Marketing is about **attracting** customers, getting them to **choose your product** or service and **keeping them** coming back for more!

I'm going to discuss the 3 key points from that definition...

1. Attracting
2. Choosing
3. Keeping

Imagine two salons next door to each other; both offering spray tans to the market described in Step1. Salon 1 has a clean glass shopfront looking into a nice-looking salon with a pretty sign and a spray-tan company logo/poster in the window; nothing fancy just average. Salon 2 has a dirty-ish window (dried up rainwater, some finger marks, etc) looking into an average salon with a worn sign, but on the window, in big bold clear letters, a sign saying ***"The Best Celebrity Spray Tans for £15 - We've been spraying for 10 years!"***

Now if you had limited funds and needed/wanted a spray tan which one would you spend your precious £15 in? I know which one I would choose but that's not the point... the point is - which one will be most '***attractive***' to the market?

Attracting
So point 1 is about what you do to attract your market... is it through affordability, glamour, quality, latest trends, cleanliness, relaxation, expertise, cheap & cheerful, branding and so on.

Use the information you have gathered in Step 1 about your largest core market and incorporate what is ***important*** to them into your salons' interior, exterior, treatment and product list and all *written and verbal communications. Attract them - stop them in their tracks by using the right words, images, colours, textures that interrupt their daily lives and bring your service to their attention.

Many salons I have visited use up prime salon wall space to display things like certificates, salon licenses, insurance, terms of business and such... please note, these things do absolutely nothing for your customers. The only people that are interested in this information are judges for professional awards, your colleagues, health & safety inspectors and the like. By law you must display your licenses and insurance but you can put them discreetly on a side wall behind some flowers! As for certificates put them in a folder ready for inspection if requested.

Use your prime salon wall space to highlight benefits and excite clients into spending their cash with you; be creative, but direct and relevant! For example... "Get your feet summer ready with our 'Callus-Off' Pedicure"

*Written communications include text on your shop window, in adverts, on leaflets, mail outs, emails, etc. Adhesive vinyl letters are a fast and inexpensive way to give a professional look to your words on walls and windows. Try www.stickair.com - they deliver worldwide and the approximate price for this example text - "Get your feet summer ready with our 'Callus-Off' Pedicure" is £18! Or search vinyl letters in Google.

<u>Choosing</u>

Would you wear your oldest most comfortable pair of pyjamas to a speed dating event... No, because it's not the appropriate attire... You will probably succeed in point 1, the attraction, but you are less likely to succeed in point 2, being chosen!

So once you have their attention...

- "Is your weave all wrong?"
- "Have your hair extensions turned into a birds nest?"
- "Had enough of patchy, orange tans?"
- "Are you paying too much for your nail extensions?"
- "Are your eyebrows out of control?"
- "Are you feeling fat, tired & unhealthy?"
- "Has winter turned you into the hairy monster?"

Then you provide content that makes them choose you...

- "Waxing, threading, electrolysis - we are hair removal experts - pop in for a free booklet"
- "Stop wasting your money in other salons and get the results you've been wanting right here, with us"
- "We have award winning weave experts at hand"
- "Free weighing and health assessments this weekend; pick up your invitation today"

- "Get our top Facialists view on the latest and best skincare products - collect your free brochure"
- "Get the tan celebrities are raving about right here"

Different things work for different markets - make your salon stand out of the crowd and be the 'chosen one' by talking directly to your customers need. Know your customers needs.

(My opinion on words versus branded posters is this - I think that powerful wording on windows; highlighting key attractions is a far more effective marketing tool than branded posters. Remember, it's Joe Bloggs you are trying to attract, not another therapist who knows the in's and out's of all the different spray tan brands - this is just my opinion!)

Keeping

Now that you've got her/him through your door, wanting to ask a question, wanting to make an appointment, wanting that tan "like in the window"... what do you do? Put that supa-dupa salon coordinator from Step 5 into action!... and then what do you do? Give her the best spray tan she's ever had!! And while she's waiting for her treatment to start there's lively music playing or tv, cold colas, fashion jewellery, sunglasses, hair accessories, magazines to look at and lots of mirrors.

Client's thinking - this place is fun, and what a great result for my tan, and what a great price, and I can't resist those earrings, they will go so well with my dress. These guys are cool and this is my kind of salon - it was made for me!

Salon is thinking - well yes, it was made for you because we were actually thinking about you when we made it... we didn't just open a salon for 'everybody'!

If you give her what she expected to get and more, you are a smart marketer and your market focus and positioning will lead to greater client acquisition and greater retention. She will keep coming back to you as long as you keep focusing on her needs.

CREATE A MARKETING STRATEGY

1 - Define your target market as in Step1.

2 - Decide on your market position and USP (unique selling point) - this means to decide how you will be perceived by your target market; cheap & cheerful, high-end, affordable quality, luxurious, contemporary, experts, etc. and how you will stand out from the rest.

3 - Create the style of your brand, salon and offer in-line with your market position.

4 - Create your window shopfront and printed material in-line with your brand.

5 - Ensure your salon team are clear about the salons market position and on-board with it's aims and direction. They must always be up-to-speed with any offers and salon targets. They are a major part of the success of this process. Maintain a happy team to maintain a quality service. (Step 4 & 5)

6 - Speak to your market through your shopfront and printed material using words and images that will attract them into your shop.

7 - Create offers that are ***relevant*** to your market. For example, there is no point offering 10% off to a market that is not price-sensitive but more interested in environment. (By-the-way, 10% off doesn't really entice anyone into making a purchase; it's overused). Importantly, keep your offers simple! Below is an example of the same offer presented in 4 ways:-

> Get a spray tan today and book your next 2 for half price
> Get a spray tan, book in advance and get next 2 for 1
> Get 3 for 2 spray tans this month
> Enjoy a free tan on us - Buy 2 get 1 free

Which one do you think works best? Also note that going with the examples in this booklet, this offer equate to £30 in the till for 30 minutes work. Remember to ensure your offers are still profitable for you - Step 3

A more high-end salon or spa could offer...
Handbag designer, Miss X will be hosting a champagne reception in our private room next Saturday - secure entry to this exclusive first viewing of her new range by booking a course of facials with us today. Alternatively purchase a £100 token today redeemable upon a treatment booking. Telephone Marie directly on 123 456 789.

8 - Decide on your methods of contacting and updating your current client list with new offers - via post, phone, text or email. Plan how many times you will use this method as overkill brings negative returns. I recommend planning your offers and communications at least 6 months in advance and contacting clients a maximum of twice a month.

9 - Advertising & PR (public relations) are a function of your overall marketing strategy. See how you get on with all of the above first before you start spending money on a PR agency or an advertising campaign. Of course now that you are more clear about who you are trying to attract (Step 1) you are more likely to use your advertising and pr budget much more effectively. For example if you are trying to reach the soon-

to-be or new mums in your area to let them know that your salon offers a unique baby area, space for buggies and pre and post pregnancy massages then you might consider advertising in the local parenting magazine. Additionally, as part of a pr campaign, you could offer one of your services to a local prize draw at a mother & baby fair or even sponsor the mother & baby fair! - say offering to pay for the printing of their leaflets in exchange for premium logo and salon details placement...

Get thinking about how and where you can place your business details in order to create awareness of your brand and product. Make this part of your marketing strategy and execute a different campaign at least 4 times a year. This can also include running competitions to becoming the 'face-of-your-salon' through local websites, radio, parties and publications.

10 - Create thorough customer service and customer complaints policies. Have clear methods of monitoring how effective your marketing and the servicing of your clients is. This is definitely part of your marketing strategy and is focused on setting targets and expectations around how many new clients you see per week or month and how many of them come back again and again. Step 4 talks a lot about methods of monitoring and assessing - this is part of marketing.

Also part of this section of the marketing strategy is clarifying your policy on rewarding regular customers; loyalty cards, points and any special discounts created to increase loyalty.

CREATE YOUR SECRET BRAND ARMY

Brand ambassadors are people who represent your brand for you wherever they go. What you want to achieve is clients so elated by their experience in your salon that they just can't help but pass on the message! Every time you watch a client leave your shop, aim for them to leave with the desire to share their experience in your salon in a positive way.

> *Nobody talks about ok; they talk about terrible or great!*

Remember that nobody talks about ok; they talk about terrible or great. So in order to create a 'secret brand army' you are going to have to provide your customers with the kind of experience that will delight them in every way!

Again, you are more likely to be able to do this properly if you focus on the overall needs of your customer first.

STEP 7
STOP | START | CONTINUE

STOP

- Confusing Marketing with Advertising and PR
- Coming up with detached, boring bits of weak advertising

START

- Creating a marketing strategy
- Understanding your customers need and attracting them based on that need
- Running advertising and pr campaigns 4 times a year
- Refreshing your shop front and salon walls with up-to-date offers and attractive statements about the benefits of visiting your shop
- Satisfying your customers need and creating enthusiastic brand ambassadors

CONTINUE

- To plan and present your business with determination and pride

STEP 8
SELL SELL SELL!

IT'S A MUST

I once met a salon owner who said to me "...retailing in the salon business is a mistake; no one comes to a salon to buy products." Well I can't tell you my horror! If you are like her then I suggest you give yourself a good shake, wake-up and listen to this... ***"Retailing is the only way to truly be successful in the salon business!!"***

Remember this booklet is about 10 steps to profitability - Other than Step 1, no other step will generate income faster than this one! Why? Because, simply put, in a business were every service requires human labour the only way to increase revenue without increasing costs is through retail.

...In a business were every service requires human labour the only way to increase revenue without increasing costs is through retail!

HOW TO SELL MORE!

Seeing is believing!

I opened my first salon completely not appreciating the importance of retail - I thought the treatments would make enough money. I soon realised this was a mistake and started trying to rectify the situation by creating displays and incentives for the team. Eventually the salon started retailing quite well, or so I thought... When I opened my second salon, I was lucky enough and through no conscious effort of my own to have two people join the team from pure retail backgrounds. Well it was phenomenal how the retail sales figures just shot up! We went from about 7% to around 30% after they joined! Yes, wow! That's what you get when you know how to sell! Of course their abilities were inspirational and therefore infectious - everyone could see that selling wasn't impossible!

If you personally have had average or limited success in retailing products then I can understand if you feel that this area of salon business is difficult - you don't *quite* get it. You find that you generally avoid the subject and look to 'blame' the lack of sales on the client type, your location, the economy... anything but you!

So first things first, remove any personal mental blocks you may have about retailing in your salon and understand that salons offer a great and unique platform from which to sell!

Learn from the best

You can learn from the experts in 2 main ways - go out there and observe how it's done or get someone to teach you...

Helping yourself
Observation is a powerful way of learning how to do it yourself! Take yourself and your team shopping... go to supermarkets, department stores, corner shops, open markets and visit popular shops on the high street. Study the product range, shop layout and the way the products have been displayed. Study the way the best retailers operate - what do they say, how do they say it?

You may have been to these places hundreds of times before as a customer, but with this mission in mind you will see them in a completely different light. Make notes about everything - what products are at eye level, which ones are not, how they are labelled, described and priced, what products are displayed together, how each sections are identified, which ones require shop assistant help and testers and which ones don't and why.

Make notes about what you consider their market and market position to be. Start to visualise how you will incorporate all you have learnt into your business.

Getting help
If you or any of your team are finding it difficult to overcome your mental block towards selling join Miss Salon on our ***1-Day Sell It! Workshop*** in London. We cover everything from choosing the right stuff for your salon to merchandising to role play - it's great fun and everyone leaves empowered and motivated to make money! Call us on 0845 643 1619 or visit www.misssalon.com. (All of our workshops will be available on DVD soon, along with the workbooks)

The key ingredients

To successfully retail in your salon you will need 4 key ingredients:-

1. Sourcing the right products
2. Effective displays - merchandising

3. Providing testers
4. Having a trained and incentivised team

1. Source the right products

Ultimately, the only way to sell more stuff is to stock the stuff your customers want to buy!! Sounds about right, right!? If you're busy stocking expensive specialist face creams and cleansers in a salon who's market is predominately the woman described in Step 1 then you are going to struggle to sell! Simple! If however you bought in a comprehensive range of fashionable affordable jewellery, displayed it properly and then put a big sign outside saying "***Amazing fashion jewellery from £2!***", you will sell much more.... and even get clients booked in from the footfall through your door. ***Try it now!***

Now I can already hear many of you saying, but my salon is special and I'm not going to sell tacky jewellery in my gorgeous salon! Again, I will say business is business and you must always remember that your salon is not for your daily viewing pleasure but for your customers - if your customers want party jewellery then that's what you should give them! If they want organic hair shampoo then that's what you give them! If they want nail rings with leopard print nails then that's what you give them! If they want biscuits and specialist teas then that's what you should give them!

Build your business around your customers needs.

Department stores and supermarkets have 'Buyers' or buying teams - these are the people who's job it is to choose (from the millions of things on offer from wholesalers) what to put in their stores. They use their experience, knowledge of their competitors, an up-to-date view of the market, market trends and market position to make the all important decisions as to what to put on their shelves! If they get it wrong, the product just won't shift!

You must put on your 'Buyer' hat and use all the information you have gathered from Step 1 and Step 7 to create a retail stock list of items that your customers and passers-by are going to want.

Creative retailing ideas I've seen... that work!

- A cafe in a salon
- An organic grocers in a cafe
- A hairdressers in a hair extension and wig shop
- Cafe in an estate agents

Have an open mind and be creative but stay focused on your target market.

2. *Effective displays - Merchandising*

Sorry to say but many salons are 'stuck in the dark ages' when it comes to displaying items for sale. Products, with brands that are generally not known to the average shopper, are placed in glass cabinets surrounded by tissue, stones, shells, glitter and empty boxes... this is **absolutely no longer acceptable**. Consumers no longer see beauty products as luxury items and expect to be able to at least *touch* an item of interest!

Merchandising is the name of this game - presenting the products in an attractive, easy-to-understand way. Just stacking shelves with no labels is not enough - you must label the items, by section, by type, by price, by ***benefits to customer***!

Visualise this power mix...

Hair salon
↓
Nice hair stations
↓
On the wall in-between each station 3 small shelves at eye level when client is seated
↓
Shelves fully loaded with shampoos, conditioners, styling stuff and so on, sectioned into hair-type
↓
Under each item is the price
↓
Next to each section is a big arrow/sign pointing to a group of products identifying key benefits, or better still talking directly to her need - Get the Leona Lewis look with this combo - Longer lasting extensions with this spray - Frizz control here! - Volume and bounce here! - Swimmers hair care - Stylists favourite here! (Use the terms/words/language that work for your market)
↓
Client sitting having hair done - products gorgeous, clear, reachable - *and* in-use by the hairdresser at the station!
↓
Client asks, "So what's that then...?"

YES YES YES!... that's all you need! Will continue after point 4

3. *Testers*

Everybody provides testers these days... imagine a MAC counter that didn't allow you to try any of the colours... Unimaginable right?

Put testers wherever clients are sitting, utilising or shopping in your salon - place testers on trays in the waiting area, put testers near stations and pedicure chairs, put testers in the changing rooms, showers and toilets - make it obvious that these items can be easily purchased.

Also remember if you are selling items to wear - jewellery, slippers, lingerie, sunglasses, kaftans, hats, bags, makeup - to have lots and lots of mirrors!

4. Training and creating incentives for your team

Ideally through great presentation, description labels and testers you can get most of your products sold with little staff involvement - this is the aim - however you must also increase the possibility of sales through a properly trained team!

So back to my power mix...

Client asks, "So what's that then...?"
↓
Hairdresser says, "This is one of my favourite products for your hair type... it blah blah blah... and creates this great finish especially when combined with the shampoo and conditioner... You should definitely use it at home every other day...
↓
Client says, "Really, cause I find that my hair goes... blah blah blah...
↓
Hairdresser is listening, responding to concerns raised and sympathising - then she reinforces her product and methods for a solution...
↓
Finish, work continues, chat about clients choice continues, magazine reading continues. Client has the opportunity to think about the items, continue to see them, continue to have them applied to hair and and and see/digest/calculate/factor-in the price of the items quietly without having to divulge her financial concerns!
↓
End of service, hairdresser says, "There you go; is that good for you... (mirror viewing, everything's great, client happy) ...I'll get your coat and which one of these would you like me to leave at the till for you?"

Even if she says no at this close, the items have registered in her brain, next time, especially if she's happy with the way her hair has turned out, she will factor in the purchase of these items... or she may even pop in to get them before her next appointment!

Why did I call it a power mix...? The correct mix of items, labels, testers, visibility, reach-ability and knowledgeable and enthusiastic staff is a power mix for selling!

For more on retailing - How to train your team, how to merchandise, how to source more stock please see the "Open Your Own Salon... The Right Way! handbook or join us on our 1-Day Sell it! Workshop. Absolutely worth every penny! Visit www.misssalon.com

STEP 8
STOP | START | CONTINUE

STOP

- Decorating your product displays as if they were museum pieces!
- Trying to sell things that your customers don't want

START

- Taking retail seriously - aim for 30% of sales
- Sourcing items for your salon like a 'Buyer' would for a department store
- Creating displays that work - reachable, touchable, clearly labelled, attractive
- Attracting people off the street to buy
- Providing product testers

CONTINUE

- To get excited every time items are sold; it's a great feeling, -inspirational and infectious and keeps the team excited about retailing!
- To try selling different things - don't stick to *same-old same-old*, keep your offers up-to-date and changing with the seasons - like the shops do!!!

STEP 9
GET ONLINE

There are over 450 million internet users across the globe, with over 30 million active users in the UK alone, so not having an online presence would be quite negligent. I realise that you are not trying to service 30 million people, but the people you are trying to reach and service *expect* you to have a website... what if I wanted to find out what your opening hours are, how much a facial is, what facials you do... must I call for this info? Mobile phones are becoming 'smartphones' and network providers are offering unlimited internet access... soon 'everyone' will be online, on the go!

But not appreciating the popularity and accessibility of the internet is not the reason why many salon owners have not put their businesses online - no, most of you haven't sorted this out because you either think it's going to be expensive and/or you don't have the time to sort out the content for the site.

Firstly, having a website is no longer an expensive proposition. There are many different solutions out there, from individual graphics designers or printing companies dedicated to providing affordable websites for small businesses, to companies that have created do-it-yourself templates for a small monthly fee. There are even the completely free options of Facebook, Myspace and eblogger where you can create interactive business pages and blogs that can at least give your salon an online presence in the meantime. Search Google for what's on offer.

My firm recommendation is to get your salon online today and there isn't a faster or cheaper way that I know of than through Mr Site - www.mrsite.com - where you can get online for as little as £20 and have full control over content!

Secondly, the issue of time and creating content... well, I think there is no time like the present to do this especially as you've just spent time reading this booklet and putting together a marketing strategy in Step 7 which includes your market, your market position and how you present yourself to the customer.

A SIMPLE SITE

There is no need to get yourself confused with all the hosting package, domain name jargon that is just additional headache for you - suffice for you to know that owning a website should not cost you more than £10 per month (and that's an expensive package). Anything above that is usually the fee charged by the designer to create your site or make regular updates.

If you purchase a do-it-yourself shopping cart template then the site can cost slightly more on a monthly basis but I wouldn't recommend those unless you are planning to seriously focus on online retail. Mr Site offers a great 'small shop' solution within the same low cost package mentioned above. The main Miss Salon website is www.misssalon.com but we loved Mr Site so much we couldn't resist buying a template and trying it out ourselves, hence we also have www.misssalonbusiness.com! Take a look at our online shop powered by Mr Site there. Keep in mind of course that we are a business-to-business operation, there are many lovely templates on offer that are much more pretty and fun.

So to start, a five-page simple website is all you need to get the important aspects of your salon message across:-

Home page

- Logo
- Name, address and telephone number
- Your big pow slogan - your USP!
- Few intro sentences saying what your salon is about
- Your big offer of the moment (the line you're using to pull people in at the moment)
- A selection of your best salon photos
- Links to Meet The Team, Treatment List, Salon Info, 10 Must-Have's

Meet the team page

Include photos of team members in action along side brief descriptions of who they are and what they are experts in! Make it sharp and relevant to the reader - they only want to know who's really good at what. There is no need for a list of certificates here, just number of years in the industry will do. Talk about the teams general philosophy; how they like to serve and give clients the best! This is also a great place to put the businesses customer service policy strap line! - ***"We make it our business to bring you the best in skin care - in the salon and at home"***

Treatment list page

This should literally be your price list online. However, here is a good place to add any positive comments clients have made about certain treatments or any comments/ suggestions therapists have made about the treatments. Bring the list to life with these added extra statements. Better than just the usual list of treatments... waxing - upper leg, lower leg, upper lip, chin, underarm, blah blah blah... boring, why not add something interesting about waxing in your salon; for example, our resident waxing expert is known for 'taking no prisoners' - ***"She get's them all!"***

(Also add more pictures - especially of actual treatments in your salon (these must look good though) - not these boring overused shots of someone having a massage!)

Salon info page

- Here put your address and contact details
- Travel map and directions
- Parking options plus other travel options
- More pictures of the salon
- Salon policies, especially with regards late arrivals, cancellations

Top 10 Must-Have's

Use this page to highlight 10 of your top products for retail - include images, prices, features and benefits... and sell them online!

MAKING MONEY ONLINE

A website is another shop front and clearly another potential revenue stream... and because it costs so little to run it only makes sense to give online retailing a go! As a salon you are already in a unique position to fulfil online orders - the stock is already in the salon - you just need to get the stuff in the post! And when business picks-up you can set specific time aside twice a week to fulfil orders.

There are many online payment solutions, however at the moment my favourite is PayPal - www.paypal.com - they take credit card and cheque payments on your behalf, saving you the trouble of complex bank integration and the worry of fraud and misuse. You can then transfer the money you earn from your PayPal account to your normal business bank account... *Easy!*

STEP 9
STOP | START | CONTINUE

STOP

- Waiting to get your salon online; it can take Google and the other search engines a while before they start to register/recognise your site so the sooner you get on there the better it is for your search engine ranking

START

- Giving your clients the option of finding relevant, reliable and flattering information about your salon online
- Creating the opportunity for increased revenue through online sales

CONTINUE

- Moving with the times!

TECHNOPHOBE ALERT!

If getting started online still sounds like a daunting task then have no fear Miss Salon can sort out the beginnings of your online presence with the following package:-

1. A fully customised Mr Site Beginners 5-page website; including advice on content, wording and image/logo manipulation for best effect. Also including an online shop of 10 items.
2. Assistance with starting a PayPal account to use in conjunction with your online shop.
3. Creating and populating a customised facebook business page or group.
4. Creating a Twitter account for your salon - one 'tweet' could let your regulars know when there is appointment availability and more!

Our designers are very particular and we always ensure that the end result looks crisp and professional, but more than that we are commercially-minded and work with you to create content that works for your market.

All this for *£450. Project usually completes in one week.
Please note, this fee does not include on-going management of the sites, but we will help you understand how you can maintain the content of your pages yourself. Email us or call! misssalon@misssalon.com | +44(0)845 643 1619 | *prices may vary*

STEP 10
STAYING IN CONTROL OF YOUR BUSINESS

Don't let all this hard work you've just done go to waste... especially when you start to see improvements in your sales! All of this will need to be maintained and monitored; that is your job as a manager owner.

SET UP ON-GOING MONITORING PROCESSES

Use a yearly planner and mark the dates out, over a 12 month period, for the following activities:-

- 6 In-house salon inspections
- 6 Training and rehearsal days
- 2 Staff performance reviews
- 1 Marketing plan for the year - including preparing what offers to have 6 months in advance
- 4 Advertising and/or pr campaigns
- 8 Retail product reviews
- 12 Cash flow updates
- 12 P&L updates
- 8 Shop front window changes
- 6 Mystery shopper visits
- 2 Major team days/nights out
- 12 Staff meetings to discuss monthly salon sales and the followings months focus
- 2 Industry exhibition visits
- 2 Client feedback forms
- 12 Website updates (there may not be any updates but at least set dates to check that the info is still correct)
- 1 (at least) holiday!!

Then just follow your plan - stick to the dates you set out. If you also work the shopfloor and have clients then make sure the dates for the jobs listed above are marked out in the appointment book - do not allow yourself to get booked up and miss doing the jobs that only you can do!

DON'T BE AFRAID TO WIN!

The principles described in this booklet work across the board from spa's to single mobile technicians, from salons on busy high streets to single treatment rooms above shops or home spas in small villages. Determining your customers need first and then providing the services and products that meet that need is the key to a profitable business.

Winning takes courage, discipline and hard work - don't fall short of winning in your venture - You can do it!

So go ahead and apply these 10-steps to your business... you will be well on your way to long-term success!

STEP 10
STOP | START | CONTINUE

STOP
- Allowing important tasks to get away without be completed

START
- Running an organised operation - be strategic, methodical and disciplined - Think *"Discipline brings excellence and excellence brings freedom"*

CONTINUE
- Being an excellent manager owner of your wonderful salon!

MORE HELP WITH YOUR BUSINESS

MISS SALON MENU *(All prices quoted here may vary)*

Books
Kick-Start Your Salon Into Profit Paperback £14.99 | e-book £10
Open Your Own Salon... The Right Way! Paperback £45 | e-book £40

Workshops (Coming soon on DVD)
Kick-Start Your Salon Into Profit! 1-Day Power Workshop £200
Open Your Own Salon The Right Way! 1-Day Workshop £150
Sell It! 1-Day Workshop £100 (25% Discount for group bookings)

Mentoring & Consulting
Miss Salon Business Mentoring™ Package £300 per month
Miss Salon Business Consulting £40 per hour or project based

Marketing (Price upon application)
Marketing Plan and Strategy
Market Research and Questionnaire
Mail Shots, Adverts and Other Customer Communications
Advertising and PR Campaigns
Online Marketing Channels (Website, Facebook, Twitter, Blogs, YouTube, MySpace, etc)

Salon Documents
Salon Health & Safety Policy Template £19.99
Salon Health & Safety Procedure Template £24.99
Sample Salon Health & Safety Induction Procedure £9.99
Sample Salon Staff Handbook and Contract of Employment £9.99
Sample Salon Staff Recruitment Interview Questions £3.99
Staff Performance Review Questionnaire £3.99
Salon Inspection Sheet £3.99

Document Creation (Price upon application)
Business Plans
Operation Manuals
Training Manuals
Business Proposals
Staff Handbooks

Available online at www.misssalon.com or telephone 0845 643 1619

KEEP UP-TO-DATE

Miss Salon Business Blog - including our diary and salon videos
www.misssalon.blogspot.com

Miss Salon Facebook - including latest images, videos, events and more
http://www.facebook.com/pages/Miss-Salon/67171720155

Miss Salon Tweets!
www.twitter.com/misssalon

Miss Salon Channel www.youtube.com/misssalon

GOOD LUCK WITH YOUR BUSINESS!

Lightning Source UK Ltd.
Milton Keynes UK
16 September 2009

143770UK00001B/7/P

9 780956 035134